KINGFISHER

First published 2010 by Kingfisher
an imprint of Macmillan Children's Books
a division of Macmillan Publishers Limited
20 New Wharf Road, London N1 9RR
Basingstoke and Oxford
Associated companies throughout the world
www.panmacmillan.com

Illustrated by Ray Bryant
Concept by Jo Connor

ISBN 978-0-7534-1956-4

Copyright © Macmillan Children's Books 2010

All rights reserved. No part of this publication may
be reproduced, stored in or introduced into a retrieval
system, or transmitted, in any form or by any means
(electronic, mechanical, photocopying, recording or
otherwise), without prior written permission of the
publisher. Any person who does any unauthorized
act in relation to this publication may be liable to
criminal prosecution and civil claims for damages.

9 8 7 6 5 4 3 2 1
TTR/1209/TWP/UNT/150GSM/C

A CIP catalogue for this book is available
from the British Library.

MORAY COUNCIL LIBRARIES & INFO.SERVICES	
20 30 15 91	
Askews	
J032.02	

WHAT'S IN THIS BOOK?

HOW...

HAVE YOU EVER ASKED YOURSELF HOW?

It's only natural to be confused by the world around us... It is a very complicated and surprising place sometimes! And you'll never understand what's going on around you unless you ask yourself 'HOW?' every now and again.

This is 'how' we have made this book.

We have travelled over the land, under the sea, up mountains, across deserts – and even into outer space – to collect up as many tricky questions as we could find...

...and we also found the answers for you!

We now invite you to come with us on our journey around the world of 'HOW', so that we can show you all the answers we discovered.

Did you know...

A dog's sense of smell can be up to a million times more sensitive than a human's.

While we were searching for all those answers, we found out some other pretty interesting things, too. We wrote them all down on these panels – so you can memorize these facts and impress your friends!

We also thought it might be fun to see how much of this shiny new knowledge you can remember – so at the back of the book, on pages 56 and 57, you'll find some Quick-Quiz questions to test you out. It's not as scary as it sounds – we promise it'll be fun. (And besides, we've given you all the answers on pages 58 and 59.)

Are you ready for this big adventure? Then let's go!

QUICK-QUIZ QUESTIONS

Did you know...

Monkeys, crocodiles, cats and other sacred animals were often mummified, too!

A mummy is a dead body that has been wrapped in bandages. Mummies from ancient Egypt lasted thousands of years. First, the insides of the body were removed and it was left to dry out for 40 days in salty stuff called natron. Then it was washed, rubbed with ointments and tightly bandaged.

HOW QUICKLY CAN YOU SAIL AROUND THE WORLD?

Did you know...

In 1960 the US Navy nuclear submarine *Triton* became the first craft to travel around the world entirely under water.

The quickest time a boat has sailed around the world without stopping is 50 days, 16 hours and 20 minutes. This record was achieved in March 2005 by French sailor Bruno Peyron and his crew of 13 on board the giant catamaran Orange 2.

Did you know...

The Sun is the closest star to Earth. The next nearest is called Proxima Centuri. The Sun's light takes 8.3 minutes to reach us, but Proxima Centuri's light takes 4.3 years!

HOW HOT IS THE SUN?

Like all stars, the Sun is a huge ball of burning gas. It is hottest in the middle, where temperatures reach 15 million°C!

Did you know...

We can't see the Earth's atmosphere because the gases in it are invisible. On Mars, the atmosphere is full of red dust, so the sky looks orange-brown.

HOW IS THE ATMOSPHERE LIKE A GREENHOUSE?

It gets very warm in a greenhouse, as the walls and roof stop heat escaping. Gases in our atmosphere trap heat in a similar way and keep the Earth warm. They are called greenhouse gases.

HOW MANY STARS ARE THERE?

There are about 1,000 billion stars in our galaxy, the Milky Way. Astronomers have worked out there are about 100 billion billion stars in around 100 billion galaxies!

Did you know...

There are four main galaxy shapes: irregular (no special shape), elliptical (egg-shaped), spiral and barred spiral. The Milky Way is a barred spiral galaxy.

HOW DO WE KNOW ABOUT THINGS IN SPACE?

Did you know...

The spacecraft Voyager 2 left Earth in 1977 and reached the planet Neptune 12 years later, in 1989.

Astronomers look through powerful telescopes to record what is happening in space. Astronauts, spacecraft and robotic vehicles also travel into space to try to discover new things.

HOW FAST DO SPACE ROCKETS GO?

Did you know...

The tallest rocket ever launched was Saturn V, which blasted the Apollo 11 spacecraft into orbit. The Apollo 11 astronauts were the first people to land on the Moon.

Rockets have to go faster than 11 kilometres per second to get into space. This works out at about 40,000 kilometres per hour. Rockets have to travel at this speed to escape the enormously strong pull of Earth's gravity.

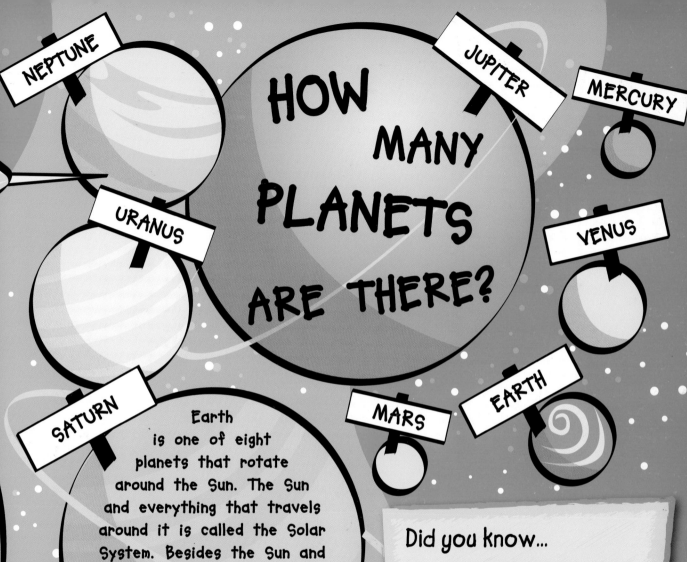

HOW MANY PLANETS ARE THERE?

NEPTUNE

JUPITER

MERCURY

URANUS

VENUS

SATURN

MARS

EARTH

Earth is one of eight planets that rotate around the Sun. The Sun and everything that travels around it is called the Solar System. Besides the Sun and the planets, the Solar System includes moons, dwarf planets, asteroids and comets.

Did you know...

Comets are like huge, dirty snowballs. Most stay on the edge of the Solar System, but a few travel close to the Sun. When the Sun's heat starts to melt them, comets grow two tails – one made of gas and one made of dust.

HOW OLD IS THE EARTH?

Did you know...

Earth is not perfectly round. It is slightly flattened at the top region (the North Pole) and the bottom region (the South Pole).

Scientists think the Earth and the Moon formed about 4,600 million years ago. Humans, though, have only been around for about 200,000 of those years.

Away from the shore, the ocean plunges to about four kilometres in most places. The deep sea is inky black and is colder than a fridge. But these are perfect conditions for some marine creatures.

HOW DEEP IS THE OCEAN?

Did you know...

The Scottish mountain Ben Nevis is 1,344 metres high. So, three of these mountains on top of each other would fit under the sea.

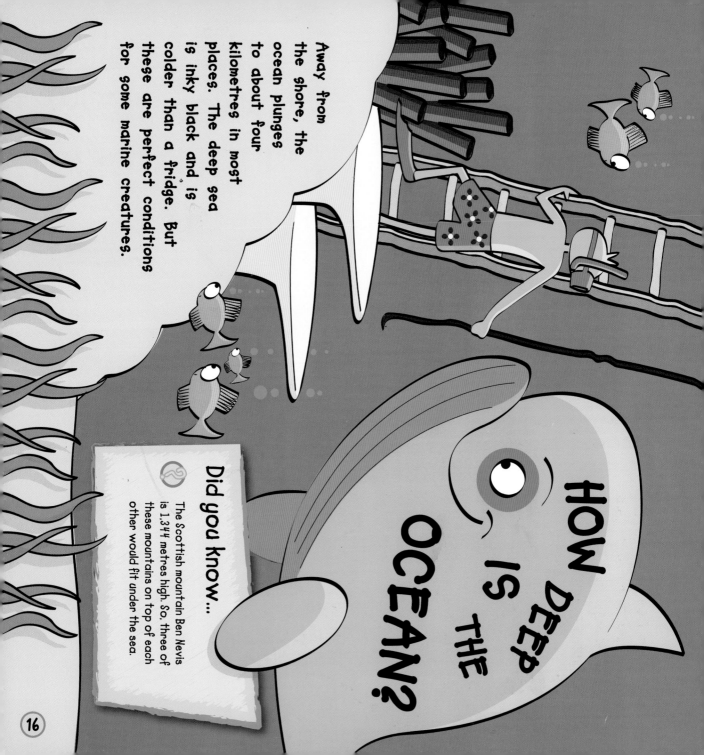

HOW HIGH IS THE SKY?

The sky is part of an invisible 'skin' of air around the Earth. This skin is called the atmosphere, and it reaches out into space for about 500 kilometres.

Did you know...

The atmosphere contains a very important gas called oxygen. All living things need oxygen to stay alive.

HOW OFTEN DOES IT RAIN IN THE RAINFOREST?

Did you know...

The world's biggest rainforest is in the Amazon in South America. This rainforest stretches for thousands of kilometres along the banks of the Amazon river.

It rains almost every day in the rainforest. The air gets hotter and hotter, until there's a heavy thunderstorm in the afternoon. After that, it's dry again.

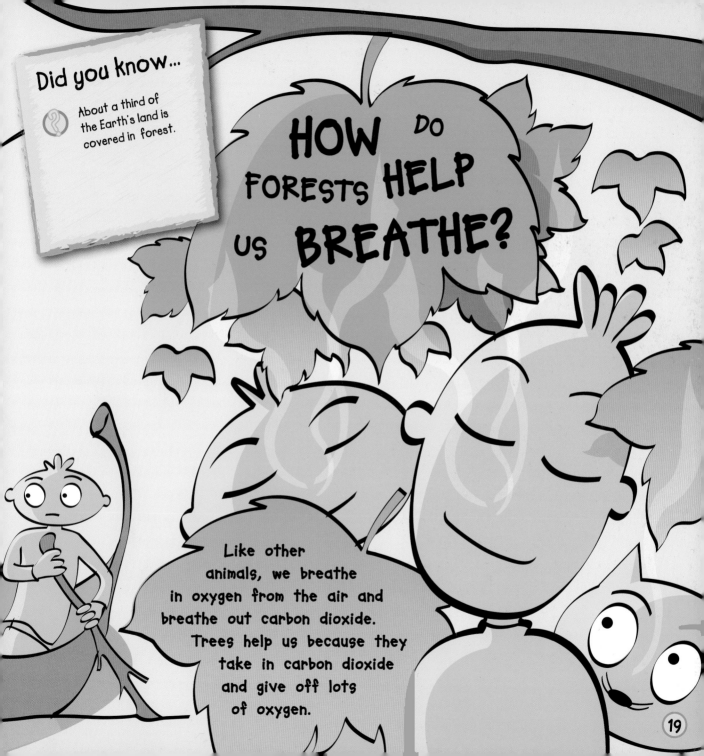

HOW DO FORESTS HELP US BREATHE?

Like other animals, we breathe in oxygen from the air and breathe out carbon dioxide. Trees help us because they take in carbon dioxide and give off lots of oxygen.

19

HOW ARE CAVES MADE?

Did you know...

Wreckers were people who shone lights to trick ships into crashing on the rocks. They stole all the valuable things on board, and hid them in caves.

Ocean waves hurl sand and rocks against a cliff face. This action by the sea slowly wears away the rock. The waves scoop out a small hollow, then a deeper hole. After a very long time, the hole is worn into a dark, damp cave.

HOW DO YOU TUNNEL THROUGH HARD ROCK?

Did you know...

Tunnels aren't just for big things like cars and trains. Smaller tunnels carry electricity cables, as well as gas, water and sewerage pipes.

Even the most powerful tunnel-boring machine (TBM) can't cope with really hard rock. Tunnel-builders have to use explosives to blast their way through.

Did you know...

Some species of shark have extra rows of teeth so, if some of their teeth wear away, they have a back-up!

HOW DO SHARKS
FIND THEIR FOOD?

Sharks can smell blood in the water hundreds of metres away. They can also sense the small amounts of electricity given off by all living things.

HOW MANY BONES DO I HAVE?

Did you know...

Bones are partly made of a hard, stony stuff called calcium. Foods such as cheese and milk contain calcium, which helps you to keep your bones strong and healthy.

Babies have about 350 bones, but adults have just over 200! This is because some of the smaller bones join together to make bigger ones as babies grow older.

HOW DO I MOVE?

Did you know...

Muscles are fixed to your bones by strong and stringy white things called tendons.

Muscles make you move by pulling your bones. To make a bone move, a muscle gets shorter and pulls the bone one way. To pull the bone back again, another muscle gets shorter.

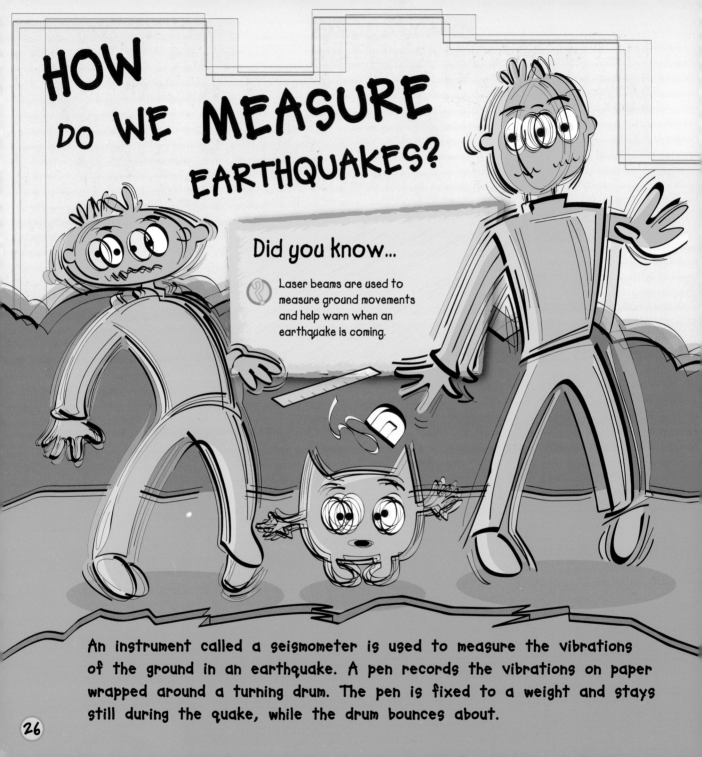

HOW DO WE MEASURE EARTHQUAKES?

Did you know...

Laser beams are used to measure ground movements and help warn when an earthquake is coming.

An instrument called a seismometer is used to measure the vibrations of the ground in an earthquake. A pen records the vibrations on paper wrapped around a turning drum. The pen is fixed to a weight and stays still during the quake, while the drum bounces about.

HOW DO WAVES GET AS TALL AS A HOUSE?

Earthquakes and volcanic eruptions can cause huge waves to form out at sea. These tsunami can travel at speeds of up to 800 kilometres an hour.

Did you know...

Some volcanoes erupt continuously. Kilauea in Hawaii has been active since 1983, throwing out five cubic metres of lava every second.

HOW DOES WATER CYCLE?

Water moves in a cycle. Tree roots soak up rain water when it falls. The water moves to the leaves and is released into the air as vapour. This rises and turns into clouds. When it rains, the cycle starts again.

Did you know...

The most rainy place in the world is Mount Waialeale in Hawaii. It rains there for about 350 days every year!

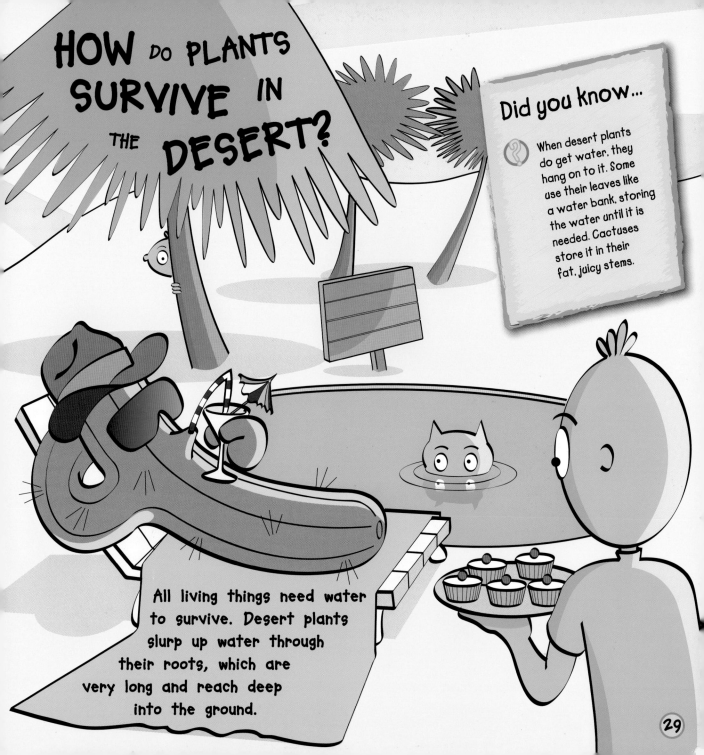

HOW DO PLANTS SURVIVE IN THE DESERT?

Did you know...

When desert plants do get water, they hang on to it. Some use their leaves like a water bank, storing the water until it is needed. Cactuses store it in their fat, juicy stems.

All living things need water to survive. Desert plants slurp up water through their roots, which are very long and reach deep into the ground.

HOW IS WIND FARMED?

Did you know...

Some power stations burn crops such as straw and elephant grass to make electricity.

The first wind-powered machines were windmills. Today, turbines are used to catch the wind at wind farms on land and out at sea. The wind is used to generate electricity.

30

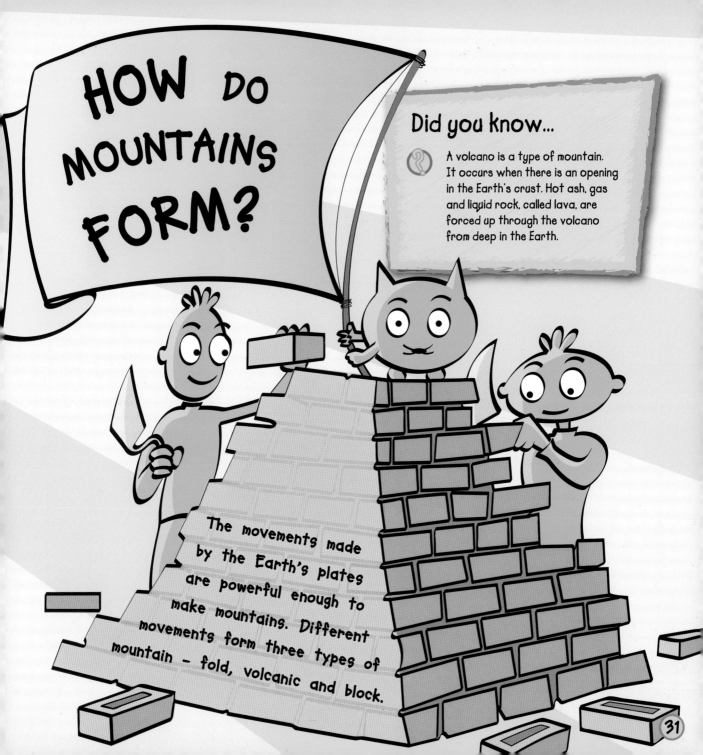

HOW DO MOUNTAINS FORM?

Did you know...

A volcano is a type of mountain. It occurs when there is an opening in the Earth's crust. Hot ash, gas and liquid rock, called lava, are forced up through the volcano from deep in the Earth.

The movements made by the Earth's plates are powerful enough to make mountains. Different movements form three types of mountain - fold, volcanic and block.

HOW DO WE KNOW WHAT DINOSAURS LOOKED LIKE?

Did you know...

Putting together a dinosaur fossil is like doing a jigsaw puzzle, and it's easy to make a mistake. Scientists first thought an Iguanodon's spike was a horn on its nose!

Scientists reconstruct a dinosaur skeleton using fossilized bones. They imagine what a dinosaur looked like by studying modern animals such as reptiles.

HOW DO WE KNOW ABOUT ANCIENT PEOPLE?

Did you know...

One of the most famous historical finds was the tomb of the Egyptian pharaoh, Tutankhamun. The tomb had lain undiscovered for more than 3,000 years!

Archaeologists study remains from the ancient world, such as buildings, tools, jewellery and coins. They look for clues in an object that might tell them how old it is, who made it and why it was found in that place.

HOW DO THINGS APPEAR ON TV?

Your TV set has an aerial to receive television signals, so the TV can turn them into sounds and pictures. These signals are sent out by tall transmitters, and bounced around the planet using satellites in orbit around Earth.

Did you know...

Television signals are carried into space by radio waves. They travel at about 300,000 kilometres an hour. This means that signals are sent up and beamed back to TV sets in just seconds!

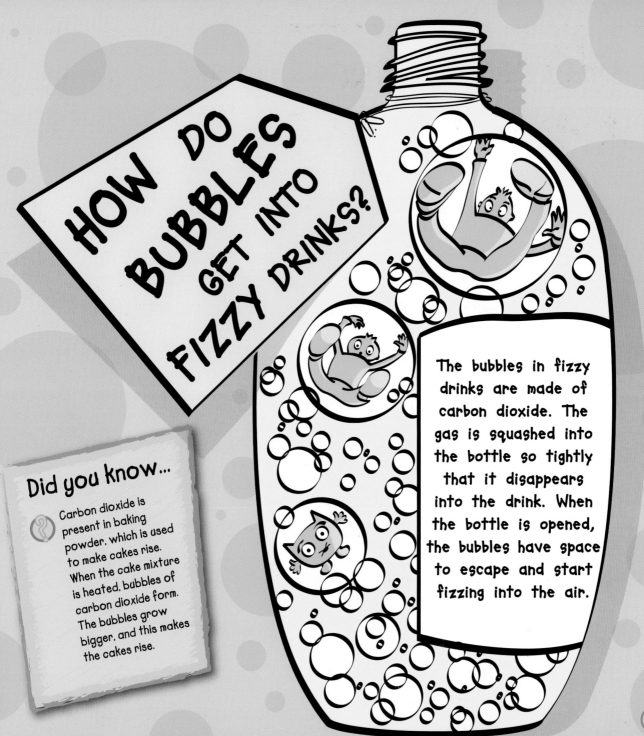

HOW DO BUBBLES GET INTO FIZZY DRINKS?

Did you know...

Carbon dioxide is present in baking powder, which is used to make cakes rise. When the cake mixture is heated, bubbles of carbon dioxide form. The bubbles grow bigger, and this makes the cakes rise.

The bubbles in fizzy drinks are made of carbon dioxide. The gas is squashed into the bottle so tightly that it disappears into the drink. When the bottle is opened, the bubbles have space to escape and start fizzing into the air.

HOW LONG DOES A TREE LIVE?

Did you know...

Trees make new wood every year and leave a tell-tale ring in their trunk. Counting the rings on a tree stump tells you how old the tree was when it was felled (cut down).

Trees grow very slowly and have long lives. Most trees live for between 100 and 200 years, but some types of pine trees are over 4,500 years old! They are some of the oldest living things on Earth.

HOW CAN YOU TELL A HORSE'S AGE?

Did you know...

Horses have to see the dentist for a check-up at least twice a year.

Horses mainly eat grass, and munching away at this tough plant food is very hard on teeth. Experts can get a good idea of a horse's age by looking at the way its teeth are wearing as it gets older.

HOW DO DIVERS KEEP WARM?

Divers wear wetsuits in cold water to help them keep warm. The wetsuits are made from rubber, which stops body heat escaping as quickly as it would normally.

Did you know...

A thin layer of water is trapped between the diver's wetsuit and their body. The diver's body heat warms this layer and the rubber wetsuit stops the heat escaping.

HOW DO ASTRONAUTS KEEP COOL?

The Sun's rays are much stronger out in space, so astronauts wear a suit of stretchy underwear to keep them cool. Tiny plastic tubes carry cool water through the underwear, taking away body heat and helping the astronaut to stay cool.

Did you know...

Space shuttles need to stay cool as well. Special tiles insulate the shuttle, and stop it getting too hot.

HOW DO SPIDERS MAKE THREADS?

Did you know...

All spiders spin silk, but they do not all make webs to catch their prey. The spitting spider catches insects by spitting a sticky gum over them.

Spiders make silk inside their bodies, drawing it out through little knobs on their bodies called spinnerets. On contact with the air, the silk sets into a thread, which the spider then weaves into a web, using its spinnerets like fingers.

40

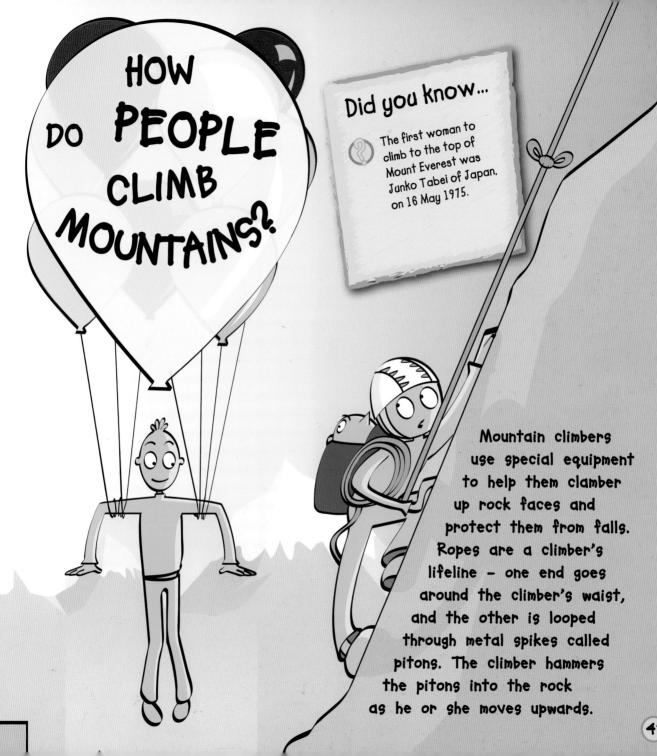

HOW DO PEOPLE CLIMB MOUNTAINS?

Did you know...

The first woman to climb to the top of Mount Everest was Junko Tabei of Japan, on 16 May 1975.

Mountain climbers use special equipment to help them clamber up rock faces and protect them from falls. Ropes are a climber's lifeline – one end goes around the climber's waist, and the other is looped through metal spikes called pitons. The climber hammers the pitons into the rock as he or she moves upwards.

HOW DO GRASSHOPPERS PLAY MUSIC?

Did you know...

Death-watch beetles like to munch through the floorboards, and they attract a mate by tapping their jaws. People once thought this knocking was a sign that someone in the house was about to die.

The male meadow grasshopper plays its body like a violin. It uses its back legs like a bow, scraping them against its wings to make a loud 'chirruping' sound. They do this to attract a mate, or warn off other males.

HOW DO SNAKES MOVE WITHOUT LEGS?

One of the ways a snake moves is by throwing its body forwards in zigzags. By pushing back against stones, it forces itself forwards and backwards.

Did you know...

Snakes can bend and twist because their backbone is made of hundreds of tiny bones, all linked together like a chain.

HOW LONG CAN A CAMEL LAST WITHOUT WATER?

Did you know...

There are two kinds of camels. Arabian camels have one hump, while the Bactrian camels of Asia have two.

Camels can survive for days without water, or for weeks if they find enough juicy plants to eat. When a camel drinks, it can gulp down 100 litres in 10 minutes.

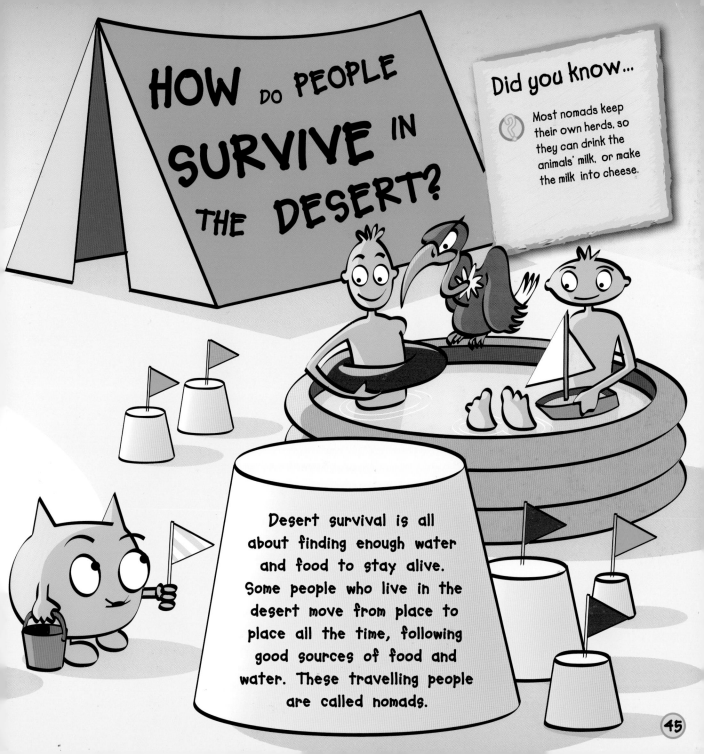

HOW DO PEOPLE SURVIVE IN THE DESERT?

Did you know...

Most nomads keep their own herds, so they can drink the animals' milk, or make the milk into cheese.

Desert survival is all about finding enough water and food to stay alive. Some people who live in the desert move from place to place all the time, following good sources of food and water. These travelling people are called nomads.

HOW DO BATS SEE IN THE DARK?

Bats can fly and find food in total darkness. They do this by using sound waves. Bats make high-pitched sounds, which bounce off solid objects and back to the bats. This means bats can avoid bumping into things in the dark.

Did you know...

Vampire bats are the only mammals that feed entirely on blood. They live in groups of about 100, and one colony can drink the blood of 25 cows in one year!

HOW DO I KNOW WHAT'S GOING ON?

Did you know...

A dog's sense of smell can be up to a million times more sensitive than a human's. This is why the police use dogs to help them detect things that are hidden from view.

You have five senses. They are sight, hearing, smell, touch and taste. Using information from your sense organs - such as your eyes, ears, nose and tongue - the brain learns about the world around you.

HOW HIGH CAN A KANGAROO HOP?

Did you know...

A flea can jump over 100 times its own height!

A large kangaroo can jump right over your head! The highest a kangaroo has ever jumped is about three metres. Their big, strong back legs help kangaroos to be such good jumpers.

HOW FAST CAN A CHEETAH RUN?

Did you know...

Cheetahs use their sharp claws to grip and push against the ground as they race along. Olympic runners have spikes on their shoes for the same reason.

A hungry cheetah can sprint faster than 100 kilometres per hour when chasing something to eat. But running this fast soon tires the cheetah out, and it has to stop to get its breath back.

HOW DO SUBMARINES SINK?

Did you know...

One of the earliest submarines was built by Dutchman Cornelius van Drebel in the 1620s. Twelve oarsmen rowed a wooden boat below the surface of the River Thames in England.

Submarines sink by making themselves too heavy to float. Water is let into special tanks, which weigh down the submarine. When the submarine needs to resurface, the water is pumped out.

HOW MUCH DOES THE BIGGEST BABY WEIGH?

Did you know...

Baby blue whales grow at an amazing 90 kilograms a day. They grow into the world's biggest creatures, weighing in at around 130 tonnes.

The blue whale gives birth to a 2,000-kilogram whopper that is already seven metres long. A human baby only weighs 3.2 kilograms at birth and is around 50 centimetres long.

HOW DO YOU RIDE ON AIR?

Did you know...

In the 1930s, planes carried 20 passengers at the most. By the 1970s, jumbo jets could seat up to 500. Today, super-jumbos carry as many as 850 people!

People ride on air every time they travel by hovercraft. The hovercraft was invented by Christopher Cockerell in 1959. He discovered that trapping a cushion of air beneath a boat lifts it up above the waves, allowing it to travel much faster.

HOW DO BIRDS FLY?

Did you know...

Hummingbirds are the only birds that can fly backwards. They can also fly fowards, sideways and upside-down.

When birds flap their wings up and down, they are pushing themselves through the air. This gets tiring after a while, so they save energy by gliding and let the air currents carry them along.

HOW DO BIRDS KNOW WHERE TO GO?

Did you know...

It gets so cold in Antarctica that some penguins migrate northwards to South America. They don't fly, of course, they swim!

In autumn, the days grow cooler and shorter. This is a signal to migrating birds that it will soon be time to leave to go somewhere warmer. They use the Sun, stars and landmarks to fly in the right direction.

Did you know...

Russia is the largest country on Earth. It covers more than one-eighth of Earth's land area, and borders 14 other countries.

HOW MANY COUNTRIES ARE THERE?

There are just under 200 official countries in the world, which have their own laws and leaders. But this number can change. This is because new countries are sometimes made. For example, a country might split up into several smaller ones.

QUICK-QUIZ QUESTIONS

1. How long does it take for the Sun's light to reach Earth?

2. Unscramble HERE US GONE SAGES to show what atmosphere gases trap heat.

3. Appoximately how many stars are there in our galaxy?

4. Why do space rockets have to travel so fast?

5. Other than the Sun and the planets, what else is in the Solar System?

6. How long have humans been on Earth?

7. What gas do all living things need to stay alive?

8. Where is the world's largest rainforest?

9. What does TBM stand for?

10. Fish breathe oxygen from water, not air. True or false?

11. What are bones partly party made of?

12. What are tendons?

13. Unscramle SEMI METEORS to show an instrument that measures earthquakes.

14. How fast can a tsunami travel?

15. Straw and elephant grasses can make electricity. True or false?

16. What are the three types of mountain?

17. Which Egyptian pharaoh's tomb lay undiscovered for more than 3,000 years?

18. Which gas creates the bubbles in fizzy drinks?

19. What age can some pine trees reach?

20. What do divers wear to help them keep warm?

21. What are the two types of camel?

22. How many senses do you have?

23. When was one of the first submarines built?

24. Unscramble CRAVE FORTH to show what travels across water quickly.

25. What is largest country in the world?

QUICK-QUIZ ANSWERS

1. 8.3 minutes.

2. HERE US GONE SAGES = greenhouse gases.

3. About 1,000 billion.

4. To escape the pull of Earth's gravity.

5. Moons, dwarf planets, asteroids and comets.

6. About 200,000 years.

7. Oxygen.

8. The Amazon Rainforest is in South America.

9. Tunnel-boring machine.

10. True.

11. A hard, stony stuff called calcium.

12. Strong, white stringy things which attach muscles to bones.

13. SEMI METEORS = seismometer.

14. Up to 800 kilometres an hour.

15. True. Some power stations burn them to make electricity.

16. Fold, volcanic and block.

17. Tutankhamun's.

18. Carbon dioxide.

19. More than 4,500 years old.

20. Wetsuits.

21. Arabian camels and Bactrian camels.

22. Five.

23. In the 1620s.

24. CRAVE FORTH = hovercraft.

25. Russia.

TRICKY WORDS

AIR CURRENT
Moving air caused by differences in temperature or air pressure.

ARCHAEOLOGIST
Someone whose job it is to find out about human history by recovering and studying remains such as buildings and clothing.

ASTEROID
An object made up of rock and metal, orbiting (travelling around) the Sun, left over from when the Solar System was formed.

ASTRONOMER
A scientist whose job it is to study the planets, stars and galaxies.

ATMOSPHERE
The layer of gases surrounding a planet. Earth's atmosphere keeps in heat from the Sun, but also keeps out many harmful rays from the Sun.

CARBON DIOXIDE
A colourless, invisible gas that animals exhale (breathe out). Plants absorb it as they grow. Carbon dioxide is also produced by burning fossil fuels, such as coal and oil.

CATAMARAN
A boat with two hulls, or bodies, joined together so that they are parallel to each other (side by side).

COMET
An object made up of ice, dust and small rocks that orbits the Sun. Unlike asteroids, comets usually have two 'tails' – one made up of dust and one of gas.

FOSSIL
The remains of a plant or creature that existed long ago. Fossils are usually formed from the hard parts of an animal or plant, such as teeth, bones or shells. They are created when, for example, animal bones sink into mud, which then gradually hardens into rock.

GALAXY
A huge system of millions or billions of stars. The stars, together with gas and dust, are held together by the force of gravity.

GRAVITY
A force of attraction between objects. This happens in space, for example, where a moon is held in orbit around a planet, because the planet is more massive.

GREENHOUSE GASES
Gases in the Earth's atmosphere that contribute to the greenhouse effect, or global warming. Greenhouse gases include carbon dioxide, nitrous oxide, methane and ozone.

HOVERCRAFT
A boat that travels across water on a cushion of air.

INSULATE
To cover with material in order to keep warm.

LAVA
Liquid rock that spurts from volcanoes or cracks in the Earth's surface.

MIGRATE
To move from one place to another according to the changing seasons.

NATRON
A type of salt found at the bottom of dried-up lakes.

ORBIT
The path of an object as it travels around something. The Earth orbits the Sun.

OXYGEN
A colourless, invisible gas in air that animals need to breathe in order to live.

PALAEONTOLOGIST
Someone whose job it is to find out about prehistoric life by studying the fossilized remains of plants and animals, such as dinosaurs.

PREY
An animal that is hunted and eaten by another animal.

SENSOR
A part of an animal's body that gathers information for a particular sense, such as taste or smell.

SEWERAGE
The system of drains used to carry sewage (human waste and waste water).

SOLAR SYSTEM
The Sun and the objects in space that orbit it, including the eight planets.

SPACE SHUTTLE
A spacecraft that carries astronauts on space missions.

SPINNERET
A spider's silk-spinning organ, usually found on the underside of their body. Most spiders have six spinnerets.

TRANSMITTER
A device that changes a signal into radio waves that can travel through space. The signal can travel long distances and can be received by a machine, such as a television.

TUNNEL-BORING MACHINE
Gigantic drill-like machines that twist and grind their way through the ground to make large tunnels.

TURBINE
A tall machine with long blades that turn in the wind to capture its energy. The wind energy is converted into electricity.

VAPOUR
A mass of tiny drops of water in the air, which appears as mist or steam.

WATER CYCLE
The 'journey' of water as it rises and turns into clouds, in the sky, and then falls back to the ground as rain.

WHERE TO FIND STUFF

Wow! What an amazing
journey! We hope you had
as much fun as we did, and learnt
many new things. Who knew there was so
much to discover about 'how'! Speaking of
'who', we can tell you that we'll soon be
going on a few more exciting journeys:

The Book Of... Why?
The Book Of... What?
The Book Of... Who?

Look out for these great books!
'Who' knows 'what' we'll discover...

See you soon!